THE SERIAL INFLUENCER

ESTABLISH CREDIBILITY, GAIN TRUST, & DRIVE PARTNERSHIPS

AKKSHADA MANIYAN

2

Contents

1: INTRODUCTION

He will win who knows when to fight and when not to fight.
-Sun Tzu

It is 2024. And the workplace has experienced significant shifts in trends and priorities in the last five years alone. The Pandemic, Return to Work, the Great Resignation, Quiet Quitting, global economic volatility, global workforce, hybrid workforce, and entry of the Gen-Z workforce are significant events shaping workplace experiences.

How are these trends connected to Influencing?

- Employee Engagement: A survey by LinkedIn showed that 70% of U.S. employees would not work at a leading company if it meant they had to tolerate a bad workplace environment. This underlines the influence of leadership and culture within the workplace.

- Leadership Development: Gallup also reports that managers account for at least 70% of the variance in employee engagement scores across business units. This highlights the pivotal role of managers in influencing employee attitudes and behaviors.

- Financial Performance: According to Gallup, organizations with high employee engagement rates are 21% more profitable than those with low engagement.

- Building for the Future: A study from the Economist Intelligence Unit found that the ability to influence is a critical skill for success in the workplace. Around 40% of respondents stated that influencing colleagues is vital to their job role.

- Collaboration: A Salesforce survey found that 86% of employees and executives cite the lack of collaboration or ineffective communications for workplace failures. This suggests that influence exercised through good communication can lead to more tremendous success.

- Negotiation: A survey by Korn Ferry revealed that 70% of professionals feel they need negotiation skills to succeed at work, indicating that the ability to influence outcomes positively is valued.

Today, the ability to influence others in the workplace reflects the changes in technology, society, and how we communicate. And the need for this skill has been heightened since the pandemic. Employees at the workplace are increasingly skeptical of traditional corporate messaging. They prefer genuine interactions and are influenced more by influential leaders and organizations that exhibit authenticity and transparency.

Some key influencing trends that successful teams, departments, and organizations incorporate are centered across three pillars:

Values-Based Influence: Especially among younger demographics, there is a growing trend where purchasing decisions are heavily influenced by a company's values and social responsibility. Organizations and leaders communicating their commitment to social or environmental causes are far more successful in influencing at scale.

Data-Driven Influence: Advances in data analytics have allowed for more targeted and personalized influence strategies. Organizations that analyze employee data to tailor their messaging predict which methods will be most effective for larger audiences. Providing data-driven content that educates, entertains, or informs is a popular way to build trust and influence.

Visual Influence: With reduced attention spans and an overload of information, visual storytelling through infographics, videos, and interactive content becomes a powerful tool to capture attention and influence others, including social media that has a strong influence at the workplace and remains a powerful method to distribute information and thereby influence at scale.

Each of the above trends leans on the broader shift towards a more interactive, personalized, and socially conscious approach to influencing others. As technology and society evolve, so will the methods and strategies for influence. And as professionals and leaders, you can survive without influencing your immediate environment consistently. This book will discuss how to practice influence in your everyday-life

and incorporate strategies to be a *Serial Influencer.*

2: THE GAP

The gap, especially for influence at the workplace, is curating influencing skills to suit the current market and economic conditions and tailoring messages for global stakeholders. Just as stakeholders and businesses have different needs, the Influencer has different needs, skillsets, and capabilities for effective influencing.

Given the diverse workforce – cross-cultural make-up, generational representation, gender, race, etc., an intentional approach to influencing is essential, now more than ever.

Even with the best intent to persuade stakeholders, Influencers might not always have the right tools or experience to process and navigate the complexities of diverse and multiple stakeholders in the current volatile business conditions. The ideal influencing toolkit will include methods to:

- Method to evaluate if a situation requires influencing.

- A new structure to understand and manage the nuances of multiple stakeholders.

- A new model to refine or upgrade your current influencing approach.

- Strategies to remain persistent.

- Tips to network for sustained influence.

- Tools for great conversations.

In short, it is the right time to enable the development of a **Serial Influencer Model** for all audiences – to help them approach continuous, scalable, impactful influence.

3: HOW TO USE THIS BOOK

Use this book to enhance your influencing strategies to become a Serial Influencer. This book aims to help you find motivation and suggest practical tips to build credibility, gain trust, and build partnerships with your stakeholders.

Chapters 1-3 will discuss the current gap concerning influencing skills as one factor in the current market and economic conditions across their global stakeholders. We will review the need to enable the development of the Influencers' Language to drive continuous scalable and impactful influence.

In Chapter 4, we will understand how influencing in the workplace has evolved. We will review the breakup of the traditional stakeholder groups into a visible primary stakeholder group and a business group that determines the overall tone and objectives of any influencing attempts.

In Chapter 5, you can assess your current influencing skills.

In Chapter 6, we will review the new Serial Influencing Model that addresses the influencing needs in the current business environments.

In Chapter 7, we will discuss the role of Awareness as part of the Serial Influencer Model in addition to the practical strategies and stakeholder analysis template you can incorporate to succeed in your influencing efforts.

In Chapter 8, we will review the role of Articulation as part of the Serial Influencer Model and the practical strategies you can incorporate to succeed in your influencing efforts.

In Chapter 9, we will discuss the role of Action as part of the Serial Influencer Model and the practical strategies and tips you can incorporate to succeed in your influencing efforts.

In Chapter 10, we will review the role of Amplification as part of the Serial Influencer Model and the practical strategies you can incorporate to succeed in your influencing efforts.

Finally, in Chapter 11, we will reassess your strengths and areas of opportunities to create action plans using the Serial Influencer Strategies.

4: Influencing at the Workplace

Influencing within the workplace often relates to the ability to affect decisions, behaviors, and outcomes among peers, leaders, and teams. There is excellent research on principles that drive influence at work. Robert B. Cialdini's book "Influence: The Psychology of Persuasion" details six universal principles centered on cultivating relationships, reducing uncertainty, and building action. These principles will all work to hone persuasion skills across all ages.

Dale Carnegie's classic "How to Win Friends and Influence People" details universal principles of effective interaction with others and persuading them to see or understand your way of thinking. Carnegie shares many suggestions for building great conversations grounded in empathy, empathy, and genuine interest in others that have worked well for the past 80 years.

To sum it up, we approach the art and science of influence as Influencers trying to impact stakeholders (individuals and groups) by cultivating relationships, driving actions, and persuading effective decisions that mutually benefit everyone involved.

Refer to the image below for two possible influence scenarios and the corresponding results based on many recommended influencing strategies.

For reference: I – represents the Influencer. And S – represents the stakeholders you are trying to influence.

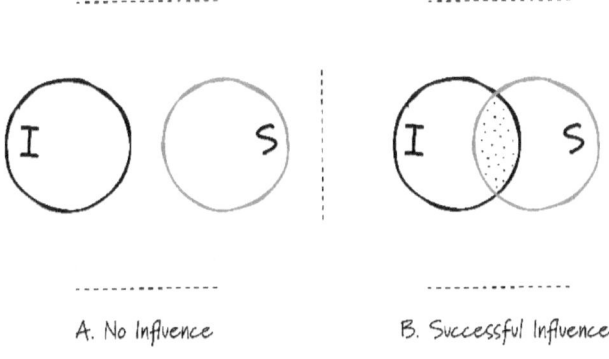

A. No Influence   B. Successful Influence

In case of a successful influence, the Influencer makes a sincere attempt to build a relationship with their stakeholders and finds enough common ground for collaborative decision-making that works in favor of everyone involved.

Alternatively, in the No Influence Scenario, the opportunity to persuade and drive any meaningful action is impossible without a conscious attempt to learn about the stakeholders' needs and interests.

The above is a straightforward, no-nonsense approach to influence. However, the approach will create setbacks in the workplace as the Influencer navigates complex dynamics associated with their stakeholder demographics, cross-cultural differences, business objectives, etc.

Common mistakes that prevent the Influencer from creating impact are:

1. Using a One-size-fits-all Approach:

Applying the same influence tactics without considering the interests and needs of multiple stakeholders can lead to strategic missteps. What works with one stakeholder might not work with another.

2. Neglecting Relationships:

Overlooking the importance of building and maintaining positive relationships across all the stakeholders or being selective with relationship management can backfire. Perceptions of favoritism can lead to resistance from a few stakeholders.

3. Working with Vested Stakeholders:

Stakeholders might misuse their authority to influence decisions in their favor. This can breed resentment, and the Influencer might face the business consequences of such decisions. It is critical to have an accountability mechanism to ensure that decisions are made for the right business reasons.

4. Not establishing Credibility and Capability:

Attempting to influence without the credibility, skills, and capability to communicate, follow up, and drive action, whether due to a history of poor judgment or inconsistent behavior, will likely fail.

5. Not establishing Transparency:

If stakeholders feel that they're not getting the complete picture or the business rationale, it can reduce buy-in and foster a climate of skepticism in the long term.

However, such scenarios can be prevented by understanding the stakeholder dynamics and the various external factors that impact solutions that you are keen to implement.

So, let's break down the above model by splitting the 'Stakeholders' and creating three groups as below:

Group 1 consists of the 'Primary Stakeholders (S) you are trying to influence and persuade. Examples at work include your manager, team members, peers, leaders, etc. You present your proposals or solutions to this group first. This group makes the initial decision to approve or implement your solutions.

Group 2 is the 'Business' (B). This is an often ignored or less talked about stakeholder group representing all the external factors such as market condition, industry trends, etc., and internal leaders representing business interests such as the C-suite and senior leadership team. It also includes the

Finance and HR teams establishing the business budget and policies. This second group set the overall tone and objectives for any influencing attempts. This group can veto any decisions the primary stakeholders make, if necessary.

The Business group is often treated as another stakeholder in a typical influencing situation. You should not take that approach. The 'Business' group is not represented by an individual or even a group of individuals. It is an invisible force that represents the tangible direction of the company's growth and future. The values and expectations of these groups should serve as a compass to steer the Influencer in the right direction as they influence others in the workplace.

Group 3 is the 'Influencer' (I). In an ideal situation, the Influencer is a habitual Influencer. A Serial Influencer, in our language. You can persuade multiple stakeholders consistently with credibility. You have earned the trust of your stakeholders as a valuable partner.

Take this scenario of Return to the Office (RTO) after the pandemic in Company A. While the organization's board was drafting policies and procedures to mandate the return to work of all employees, the department leaders and managers were silently divided on their agreement or disagreement with this mandate out of fear of retaliation. However, most employees were actively voicing their dissatisfaction over social media and company forums, further antagonizing the leadership team. This is a classic example of weak influence, limiting the possibility of any meaningful action or collaboration between the different groups.

For reference: I — represents the Influencer. And PS — represents Group 1, your Primary Stakeholders and B represents the Business (Group 2).

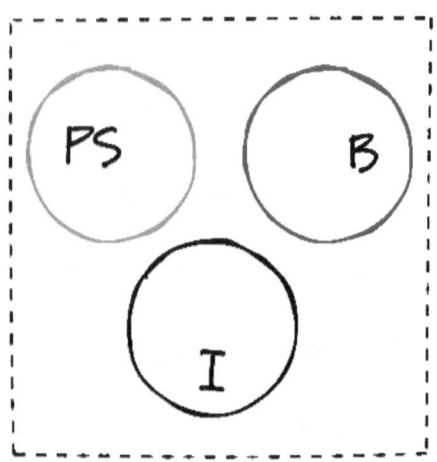

As the Influencer, consider the following questions:

- Do I have adequate resources to influence this situation with the multiple layers of decision-makers? Can one person or community affect change?

- How can I leverage data-driven, value-based, and visual influence styles to persuade stakeholders?

- What process can I follow to influence? (Upcoming sections)

When the stakeholders or business environment prevents or discourages influencing attempts, the business might have long-term consequences as below:

- Dissatisfied and unhappy employees or leaders across all three groups.

- Disengaged employees impacting performance, productivity, and retention.

- Low trust towards the leadership team without a clear demonstration of support.

- Poor company branding in online communities and social media.

- Disempowered employee groups that might think twice before trying to voice their opinions in any setting.

Let's review another scenario! Paul is interested in gaining a new AWS Professional Certification. His newly joined manager, Tara, is committed to supporting his development goals and has approved sponsoring the certification. However, given the current economic conditions, the business leadership team (including Finance and HR) declined to approve this request. The leadership team was concerned that this approval would trigger similar requests from other teams, and there needed to be a plan to address large-scale requests.

Tara feels embarrassed that her decision was questioned over what she perceives as an insignificant request. Moreover, she had budgeted 5% for learning initiatives for this financial year. She had not experienced such roadblocks in her previous stints. Paul has lost confidence in Tara's capabilities and leadership. He is questioning whether this company is right for him. This situation is an instance of Missed Influence Opportunity where everyone involved is left with a negative experience when common goals are unmet.

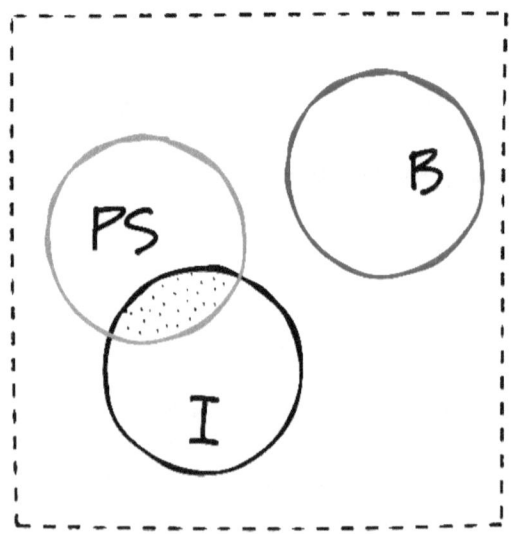

The long-term business concerns as a result of this scenario include:

- Mixed employee messaging might lead to poor morale and retention concerns, if left unaddressed.

- A disempowered leadership team might reduce engagement and trust in the organization.

- Poor manager experience might lead to retention and productivity challenges.

How about when the Business Delivery team leads and managers delegate new process mapping work to you and your team in addition to the existing projects? You don't accept this task given your limited bandwidth to support additional projects of this nature and because the Business Teams have the required capabilities to complete this task without this delegation. Moreover, the new business process expects the Business Delivery team (your stakeholders) to take ownership of such tasks. You are now expected to influence the Delivery team to accept your decision to decline the new work.

This above situation is tricky to navigate. It is also a common concern that most Support functions like IT, HR, Marketing, etc. often experience. The Influencer might over-index on the business leadership's decision to reject such a request and antagonize the client stakeholders, which might cause friction as they continue collaborating with the Delivery team on existing projects. Or the Influencer can accept the delegation by ignoring the business process and overburdening their team with more work, in addition to setting a bad precedent for the future.

However, it is possible to influence the Delivery team in this instance through the new model we will propose in the upcoming chapters.

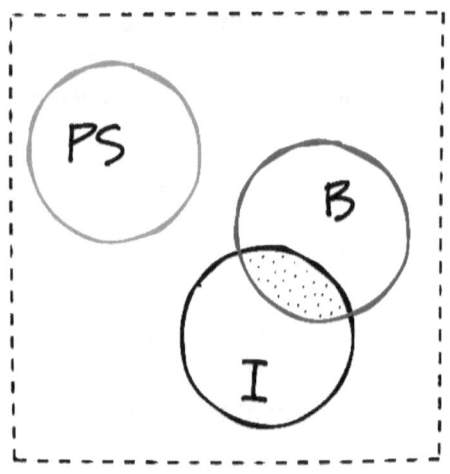

In such scenarios, the stakeholders might feel

excluded from the partnership between the

Influencer and their more extensive network group.

Influencers should pay attention to the considerations

below as they strategize their approach.

- Stakeholders might perceive a need for more transparency in the Influencer' approach. Plan for more open and candid communication.

- Stakeholders might reduce the scope for future collaboration and communication with stakeholders as trust might get eroded. Be proactive with your communication.

- It'll take time to resolve such situations. Take care to approach it tactfully and follow up with the stakeholders to build trust and partnership.

Another instance is when the department managers and business leaders are satisfied with the current project management tool. As the new IT Lead, you want to propose a new project management tool for better ticket tracking and monitoring. Change is not always easy, especially when the current process might not be troublesome for some of the workforce. How can you use the right influencing strategy to attempt change management?

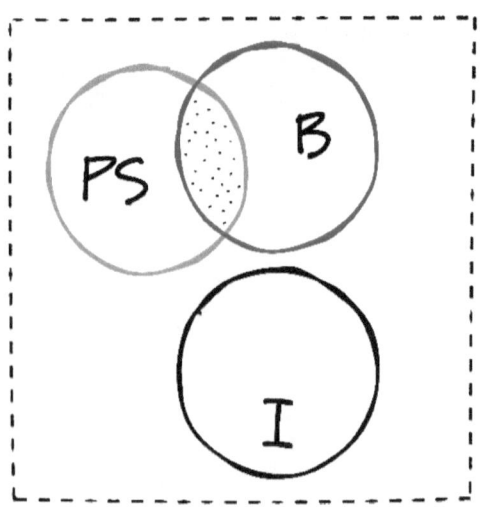

In such scenarios, the stakeholders might have more power given the support of the business as well. Influencers need a tactful strategy to address this scenario. They can start by:

- Managing their emotions as they try to influence others.

- Adapting their strategy to meet the larger audiences' needs.

- Adopting the Influencers' Language to gain traction.

Continue reading to learn more!

INFLUENCING AT THE WORKPLACE TAKEAWAYS:

❖ In case of a successful influence, the Influencer makes a sincere attempt to build a relationship with their stakeholders and finds enough common ground for collaborative decision-making that works in favor of everyone involved.

❖ Alternatively, in the No Influence Scenario, the opportunity to persuade and drive any meaningful action is impossible without a conscious attempt to learn about the stakeholders' needs and interests.

❖ Common mistakes that prevent the Influencer from creating impact are using a one-size-fits-all approach, neglecting relationships, working with vested stakeholders, not establishing credibility and capability, and not establishing transparency.

❖ To be a Serial Influencer, split your stakeholders into two groups. Group 1 consists of the 'Primary Stakeholders you are trying to influence and persuade. And Group 2 is the 'Business' representing all the external factors such as market conditions, industry trends, etc., and internal leaders representing business interests.

5: Assess your Influence Skills

Use the context of your current role and respond to these statements below by examining your collective experience with your group of stakeholders.

Select the response (1 – strongly agree and 4 – strongly disagree) that best describes your answer based on the instructions provided for each question. Add your scores at the end.

Also, analyze the overall score you received across each section. Place a checkmark if you are comfortable with your scores across each section. Place a question mark if you want to focus on that particular section.

Assessment	1-4	✓/?
I seek multiple perspectives before finding a solution for my stakeholders.		
I know my stakeholders' superpowers.		
I know of my stakeholders' constraints and challenges.		
I know the business problem I am trying to solve.		
I find it challenging to get time on my stakeholders' calendars.		
My stakeholders view me as a subject matter expert in my related field.		
I have data to support my solution(s).		
My stakeholders are aligned with the rationale and benefits of my solution(s).		
I have a project plan to support my solution(s).		
My stakeholders are in sync with the short- and long-term vision of my solution(s).		
I regularly follow up with my stakeholders to update them on the progress.		
I seek and act on the feedback I receive from my stakeholders.		
My stakeholders collaborate with me on future projects and initiatives.		
I learn from my successes and failures.		
I am proactive in finding solutions for my stakeholders' business challenges.		
I am a known subject matter expert in my field across the company.		

If you scored a <u>64</u>, you're doing an excellent job of influencing your stakeholders. You can drive meaningful impact, partner effectively, and scale your solutions for your stakeholders and business as needed. As the next step, consider sampling the stakeholders you work with to complete this assessment about you and see what they think!

A score between <u>50 and 63</u> means you are good at influencing but developing new skills will help you get better at partnering with your stakeholders to drive impactful solutions.

A score between <u>30 and 49</u> indicates an opportunity to make significant investments to gain influencing skills and techniques.

Anything below <u>30</u> reveals that you are most likely working in silos without making much progress towards building partnership with your stakeholders.

Also, analyze the overall score you received across each section. To improve your **Serial Influencing** skills refer to the action plans listed in the chapters below.

- Section 1: Awareness

- Section 2: Articulation

- Section 3: Action

- Section 4: Amplification

6: Serial Influencing Model

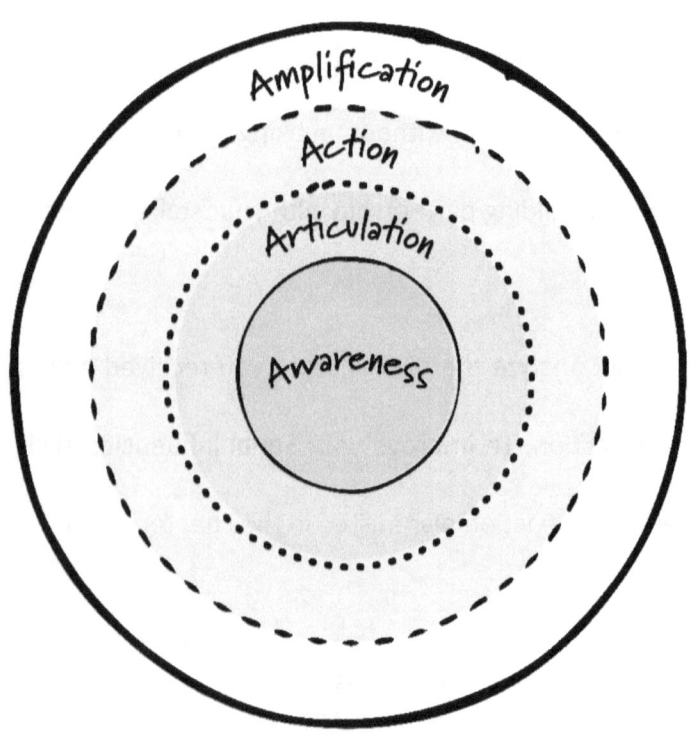

7: Awareness

'Awareness' is the first step towards building your Influencer's language. And we're not discussing being a one-time influence wonder; instead, becoming a **Serial Influencer**. To be a successful Serial Influencer, raising awareness is table stakes. And it is not restricted to only you, the Influencer. It extends to all your stakeholders, and the process of influencing will only be successful when factoring in the business needs and expectations. Let's dive deep to understand awareness from the lens of:

The Influencer (you!)

We are not naturally programmed to pause, understand, and label the emotions that we are experiencing at any given time. Emotional reactions occur at lightning speed, and before we know it, we have communicated our response to any situation both verbally and nonverbally. And most likely, we are experiencing the aftermath of our positive and negative reactions. Given the speed at which most interactions happen, **we hardly stop to acknowledge the impact of our emotions**.

We're not all natural observers; the challenge is finding a genuine methodology to reflect on your approach. To understand what you do well, what motivates and drives you, and more importantly, what triggers you? Besides processing your emotions, practicing self-awareness will also identify insights about yourself to help plan for the influencing process.

Use the questions below to understand your motivation and needs to plan for an effective influencing process.

— Does the situation need an influence?

— Should you even influence?

— Do you have the skills to influence in the situation?

— If not, how can you address the gap?

Ultimately, **self-awareness is a forcing function** that will enable you to pause and pay attention to what is happening around you and within you. It also paves the path to learning about what needs to occur in an environment you have little control or understanding.

The Stakeholders

Influencing is not a single-player game. It is a **dynamic activity with multiple stakeholders**. To set up for success, you need to understand not only your motivation and your needs but also that of your stakeholders. Some key questions Influencer should consider regarding stakeholders while preparing for effective influencing are:

— Who are the stakeholders?

— What do you know about the stakeholders' networks?

- Are the stakeholders invested or even interested in being influenced?

- Can you identify the stakeholders' behavioral and communication styles?

- Why should the stakeholders care about your idea?

The Business

Influencing is further complicated in today's world, where there are layers of complexities and nuances from a cultural, generational, and industry lens. The volatile economic condition has impacted the global marketplace. Organizations are still trying to grapple with the ever-changing ways of working. How Influencers factor business dynamics also plays a huge role in Serial Influencing. While business decisions may not always play a direct role in individual influencing goals, it is wise to weave the interests of the business into the influencing approach.

Some questions to consider for effective influence from the perspective of the business lens:

— What business problem are you solving?

— Are you aware of the current market/industry trends?

— Why should the business invest in your goals?

Without awareness, influence is impossible. You will be setting yourself up to fail without understanding the motivators and drivers of a large group of stakeholders. Be prepared to learn about the people around you as it will make you much more capable and skilled, establish credibility, and gain trust across the board.

The best part about raising awareness is that this exercise is highly personal. You own it completely end to end. It requires commitment to address the gaps, but more importantly, it needs a lot of honesty to accept the current situation and navigate towards the future.

Raising awareness is the first courageous step that you are taking towards influencing. Knowing yourself and understanding your environment to bring out your best version is an art. It comes with intentional practice and commitment.

SERIAL INFLUENCERS' STRATEGIES TO PRACTICE AWARENESS

1. NAME THE EMOTIONS

We often tend to oversimplify our emotions. For instance, using terms such as happy or sad to describe our experiences with workplace interactions is normal. However, we rarely understand the deeper emotions that might be connected to the happiness or sadness we often refer to.

Being fully aware of the emotions you are experiencing without passing judgment requires deep reflection that might also need you to lean into a space of discomfort. It might be easy and even a shortcut to mask your deeper emotions with generic labels. But, once you name your emotions accurately, you can address or confront the real issue. As an Influencer, this experience will help you handle various influencing scenarios deliberately and thoughtfully.

Let's review a scenario. Tara is in a meeting with her peers and cross-functional team members to address the delays to the production run rate of a new product. Many team members have vetoed her ideas to improve the run rate, disregarded them, and even ridiculed them. As the meeting ended with no clear next steps or solutions, Tara leaves the meeting room extremely angry, making her displeasure evident to all in the room.

In this case, Tara was visibly angry with a flushed and tense face. However, Tara was probably also experiencing other emotions, such as:

— Frustration with delays in the project plans

— Shock and a sense of victimization because of the ridicule she experienced.

— Irritation with the team's lethargic inaction.

Many other possible deeper emotions will remain unidentified as Tara labels her emotion as 'Anger.' Naming them will help Tara address the positive and negative consequences of that meeting. It'll allow her to comprehend the complete picture as she plans for the next steps; whether following up with the action plan or even addressing her peers about their behavior.

Naming the right emotions is not a mere vocabulary test but the first step in acknowledging the environment (people and situations) and our natural response. Being aware of the spectrum and intensity of our emotions will help us set the right goals for any situation.

Consider this activity to better label and name your emotions:

— *Set aside time towards the end of each week (15 to 20 minutes) to write about your emotional experiences from the previous week. Writing has a lot of innate healing power as it declutters your mind and provides a* therapeutic effect as you translate your thoughts and feelings into words.

— Highlight the emotions you have listed and expand your emotional vocabulary to understand the intensity of the emotions better. Reflect upon events to address the underlying emotions that you might be masking.

— Start observing the patterns in your emotions, which will help you understand your tendencies and default emotions.

— Observe the physical reactions such as feeling flushed or experiencing a faster heart rate/pace of breathing, tense muscles, etc. Learning to spot physical reactions is a great cue to be aware and name your emotions.

— *Continue this practice for three months.*

— *Reflect and learn about the emotions you have uncovered in the last three months and congratulate yourself on your discoveries in labeling your emotions.*

Once you've started this practice for yourself, start applying this to your stakeholders as well. Learning about the root cause of your stakeholders' emotions can also help you tailor your messages and solutions.

2. KNOW YOUR CORE VALUES

In the regular hustle of workplace dynamics, you might mindlessly follow the norm established by the company culture or a few peers and leaders. Stop.

Stop and consider the values and beliefs that you once envisioned for yourself. If you have yet to envision such a vision, you can create it now.

Ideally, your core values are behaviors and actions that reflect your motivation and your drivers. Your values make you get out of bed to begin each day with enthusiasm and purpose. Your values make you feel satisfied, grateful, and thankful at the end of each day.

Your core values also act as the compass to determine if you need to influence in any situation. **Your approach to influencing should resonate with your core values for it to be authentic and even ethical.** Why bother investing time and effort in any activity that might directly contradict your core belief system?

To create your core values, think of the most meaningful moments in your life. Now answer the following questions:

— Who did you share them with? Why were they the most meaningful moments? Why do you want to recreate them?

— What were some of your worst life experiences? Why do they bother you still?

What behaviors from these experiences
bothered you the most?

— Have you experienced any inspiring moments
recently? Or who has inspired you recently?
Are there any behaviors you admire in these
people or stories? List these behaviors.

— What are your pet peeves? What makes you
angry or disappointed?

— If you could create an ideal day at work, how
would that be? How would you or your
coworkers treat each other?

As you answer some of the questions above, you
will start seeing overlapping behaviors that you see in
yourself and want to see in others. Identify these

overlapping repetitive behaviors and experiences. They are your core values.

Examples of core values include:

— Be Humble and Grateful

— Empower Others

— Place Family First

— Practice Well-being

— Invest in Learning & Development

— Be Curious and Open-minded

— Embrace Adaptability

When you live by your core values, you also know your non-negotiables. You are setting yourself up for better emotional health, which greatly unlocks your potential at work. Bringing your authentic self to work and elsewhere will provide you with a sense of accomplishment and purpose. Influencing through your authentic core values will only motivate you to practice it regularly and attain the status of being a *Serial Influencer*.

And now, the tricky part. Review your core values periodically or before influencing, and consider the following:

— Are you still staying true to your core values?

— Will influence in this situation support or conflict with your core values?

— Are you proud of the results of your influence?

3. IDENTIFY YOUR NICHE

While you may want to influence various areas, starting with a specific niche where you have the expertise, passion, and a unique perspective is essential. The first time you begin to influence anybody, you start with zero credibility, trust, and partnership. Therefore, approaching any influencing scenario by demonstrating the value you bring with your expertise, experience, or past contributions is critical.

In short, your niche expertise becomes your value proposition to the stakeholders. More importantly, if your niche skills, passion, and expertise are one-of-a-kind, or they fill a business gap or the lack of expertise amongst stakeholders, they become an invaluable asset in any influencing approach.

You can demonstrate your niche skills by:

— Speaking authentically about your knowledge at every opportunity with a diverse audience.

— Encouraging discussions to drive curiosity on your niche topic.

— Publishing articles, books, and newsletters on your topic.

— Getting on a podcast. Talk, talk, and talk!

— Generating followership through thought leadership on social media.

— Collaborating with other like-minded experts to expand your circle of influence.

— Being available to answer questions that demonstrate your expertise and passion. It also highlights your commitment to developing others.

As an Influencer, it's essential to demonstrate or bring forward your expert skills to help accomplish the overlapping goals of stakeholders and the company. Additionally, Influencers must proactively research the niche skills the business stakeholders require.

For instance, as an Influencer, you might bring an excellent sales strategy concerning 'farming' existing client accounts. Your experience maintaining exceptional client relationships has led to successful metrics and revenue generation in adding business with existing customers. However, the need of the company or the stakeholders might be 'hunting' sales expertise where they expect you to generate revenue with potential new labels and brands. In such a scenario, the Influencer needs to consider if they have the right expertise, perspective, and experience to drive the needs of the business. If not, reflect on how they can adapt and learn to meet the needs of the stakeholders and the company.

Going in with an exaggerated value of one's niche skills can only lead to disappointment and break trust with their stakeholders.

4. SPEAK TO A NEUTRAL THIRD-PARTY

It is easy to get confused or lost when multiple dynamics and stakeholders are in the mix. Find a neutral third party who can help you declutter your thought process. Seek someone who can understand and appreciate your core values. Speak to someone who understands your drivers and your motivations. More importantly, **talk to someone disconnected from the situation to avoid biases or conflicts of interest.**

Talking to someone might help you process a large amount of information and prioritize the most crucial point. Leverage this person as a sounding board to whom you can articulate your logic and approach when influencing any scenario. Discuss what you perceive as the needs of the stakeholders and the business — and validate the same. **The neutral third party can act as a devil's advocate to help you expand your sense of awareness.** Reach out to such a person only if you can listen keenly to new perspectives, which might teach you new ways to customize and curate your influence strategy.

Include the following question to guide your discussions with the neutral third party.

— What are the advantages of your proposal?

— What are the business needs, and does your approach solve any business problems?

— Is it the right time to bring up this topic or project?

— Are you prioritizing the correct agenda and factoring in the right audience?

— Do you have a good understanding of the stakeholders and their needs?

— What can you be more aware of, especially your emotional reactions and the impact it might have on the stakeholders?

— What else should you consider or factor as part of your solution?

5. OBSERVE NONVERBAL CUES

People are constantly communicating. We can glean a lot of information about how people interact verbally and nonverbally, as communication is more than words. Nonverbal cues – such as facial expressions, gestures, body language, and eye contact – play an essential role in understanding and interacting with others.

Observing and understanding non-verbal cues can be daunting. As the first step, establish baselines, as cultural norms dictate different baselines for resting behavior. **Practice observing nonverbal behavior in multiple settings** to understand the deltas your stakeholders might demonstrate.

Nonverbal cues also apply to you, the Influencer. In line with some of the previous awareness strategies of talking to a neutral third party or keeping track of your emotions, **pay attention or seek feedback on how you demonstrate your emotions**. Notice your body language - are you crossing your arms, fidgeting, rolling your eyes, not smiling, or smiling too much?

Observing nonverbal cues takes practice. Start your observations without jumping to conclusions. A single nonverbal cue will not paint the whole picture; consider the entire cluster of behaviors over a period before interpreting their intent. If you're unsure about the meaning of a nonverbal cue, ask open-ended questions to confirm if you have understood it in the right context.

Let me share an example of a nonverbal cue I spotted with a stakeholder early in our interactions. This was during the pandemic when most meetings were conducted over video. I noticed that Sam often broke eye contact and turned his attention to the point above his screen for a couple of seconds before directing his attention back to me. He was calm, polite, and even friendly, but I often noticed this pattern, especially after he disagreed with me.

I confirmed my reading by being persistent (and polite) with my follow-up questions. I asked Sam questions like:

— What is my solution missing?

— What other factors and constraints do I
   need to consider?

— What can I change?

— What will make this better?

— How can I make my solution resonate
   better with the intended audience?

Sam's intention might have been to empower me to make independent decisions or avoid conflict. My persistence won him over as I took a conscious approach to asking for and incorporating his input. This approach encouraged him to share alternate ideas and suggestions. I altered my tone to ensure that Sam didn't feel my ideas were final and that I still welcomed his contributions.

Remember that nonverbal cues can vary widely across cultures, and what might signify in one culture might mean something entirely different in another. This observation requires practicing sensitivity and awareness of cultural differences.

6. WALK IN THEIR SHOES.

There are multiple ways to understand your stakeholders' perspective and universe. Start with a 'walk in the shoes' activity by asking them if you can shadow them for a few days or even a few meetings. Spend more time in their world to understand their constraints, business pressure, and motivation. Stay silent. **Be a shadow to learn more about what truly drives your stakeholders' behaviors and decisions.**

Most Fortune 100 companies mandate such talent mobility programs before senior-level promotions to prepare incoming leaders to succeed early. I was part of a 'walk in their shoes' program at Amazon, where I experienced employees' lives across various roles in the Amazon Warehouse. I excitedly donned the uniform vest and punched in to mark my entry. I worked every single role in the warehouse over the next few days. This included scanning, sorting, and arranging the merchandise, running QA checks, packing boxes, adding labels, and ensuring the products reached the delivery van. I packed an entire delivery vehicle – it took me 6 hours! I accompanied the drivers as they made the delivery and shadowed customer service calls to understand how to manage complaints.

This 5-day program gave me an appreciation of the story behind every delivery box I receive from Amazon - the challenges, constraints, pressure, and deadlines associated with each of them. At the end of 5 days, I received the full picture of the employees, managers, and the business needs. I gained the confidence to design the right learning experience for optimal adoption and consumption.

Another way to 'walk in their shoes' is by asking good questions. The ability to ask good questions paves the way to great relationships. Good questions indicate genuine curiosity and ensure a good back-and-forth exchange with your stakeholders. Knowing how to kickstart a conversation, how to continue a conversation, and how to bring life into a conversation are true skills that come with intentional practice. Always have a pipeline of questions that will help you continue to keep a conversation going, providing you an opportunity to learn more about your stakeholders.

Examples of such questions include:

— What's an ideal day for you?

— What's most important to you in your 'business' or 'p, ' t' or 'team'?

— What's a priority for you now?

— What are your top 3 strengths?

— Who is your inspiration?

— Tell me about your star team member.

— What was your biggest accomplishment this year? So far?

— What was your takeaway from this 'project' or 'experience'?

— What worries you most about your job?

— How can I support you now?

— What would you have done differently in

   _____ instance?

— How can I support you now?

   Don't be disheartened if you do not have the opportunity to shadow or ask questions. You can still leverage all opportunities to be a silent observer in existing interactions to observe how your stakeholders treat their team members and how they interact in their own environment.

7. INVEST IN A SOPHISTICATED PERSONALITY ASSESSMENT TOOL

Personality assessment tools can help you understand yourself and your stakeholders. It can also be a big blocker if you end up selecting a tool that is probably not high in validity (the degree to which a measurement instrument or research study accurately measures what it is supposed to measure or tests what it is supposed to test) and reliability (the degree to which a measurement instrument or research study produces consistent and stable results over time, across different observers or raters, or under different conditions). As the first step, **select a personality assessment instrument such as the Hogan or Birkman with high validity and reliability scores.**

Most research indicates that your personality is set around early adolescence. But most people don't pause to consider our default behaviors and reactions or spend little time considering the rationale and logic behind them. Personality assessment tools provide an opportunity to look into the mirror and understand the impact of emotions and behaviors at the workplace.

As an Influencer, you can use personality assessments to gain insights into your clients' behavioral patterns, preferences, and tendencies and better understand their strengths and weaknesses. These insights can help you gain awareness of your areas of opportunities in any interactions or influencing situations.

For instance, the Hogan Assessment tool measures how behaviors manifest at the workplace and how people perceive the same behaviors. This is a valuable insight for all Influencers. Likely, someone with high scores on standards, structure, and perfection might be perceived as a micromanager by others. Similarly, someone with a high score on empathy and sociability might appear as a people pleaser.

Perception is the reality in most cases, and insights from such tools can help Influencers plan to fix both the perceptions of the stakeholders and the reality of their default behaviors.

8. STAKEHOLDER ANALYSIS

Understanding your stakeholders plays a significant role in the success of your influencing strategy or business outcome. To begin with, start listing your stakeholders. And I mean ALL your stakeholders. This includes people who will have any interest in your project or proposal. This includes stakeholders who are internal to the company or external, like vendors, clients, or contractors.

Understand the role and level of influence of each stakeholder. Are they supporters, opponents, skeptics, champions, neutral observers, etc.? Knowing these details will enable you to plan for the customization of your influencing strategies across each of these groups. Additionally, the most important thing to evaluate is the interest level of your stakeholders. Will they actively endorse you by supporting your ideas publicly or act as a blocker by providing more resistance to neutralize any other influence attempts?

Every one of your stakeholders might have a different potential impact on your proposal or project. It could be positive. It could be damaging. Or it could be insignificant. The challenge is knowing the extent of each stakeholder's power in any scenario. Your stakeholders might have access to all the resources such as people, money, or access to systems and hold positions of authority in addition to having deep subject matter expertise. Your stakeholders might have the power to make the final decision or have extensive connections with people and networks that make the decision.

Assess stakeholder dynamics constantly until it becomes second nature. Observe your stakeholders and keep an open communication channel to understand what drives or motivates your various stakeholder groups.

Pay attention to how the stakeholders interact with each other. Leverage the power of networks to influence and gain more buy-in for your project. For instance, influencing is a number game, where some stakeholders might bandwagon if an initial group strongly supports your proposal or project.

Stakeholder analysis now is not a one-time task but an ongoing process. Adjust the approach periodically to be a Serial Influencer. Use this sample stakeholder analysis template to understand the drivers and motivations of your stakeholders. This will help you plan and draft the articulation strategy as the next steps.

Stakeholder Name: _____

With one of your targeted stakeholders in mind., answer the questions below.

What is your objective?

Is there overlap?

Y/N?

What is their objective?

Influence — Awareness Prep

Agenda/Objective

What groups are they apart of?

(Circle one):   Endorse   or   Blocker

Interest/Engagement

Very Unlikely   Unlikely   Likely   Likely

Based on observations...

What are their core values?

How extensive is their network?

What desicion making power do they have?

What resources (money, people, systems) do they have?

9. CONNECT THE DOTS

There is always a pattern. Are you pausing and reflecting enough to make sense of the patterns of the people and environment around you? Use the templates, cheat sheets, and questionnaires as often as possible. Observe and learn about your stakeholders. Your insights will create additional data points or insights.

Influence is all about connecting various insights. Are you able to successfully identify and connect all the relevant insights? And connect the insights that lead to meaningful and impactful decisions that support you as a Serial Influencer.

Awareness Takeaways:

❖ 'Awareness' is the first step towards becoming a Serial Influencer.

❖ Self-awareness is a forcing function that will enable you to pause and pay attention to what is happening around you and within you.

❖ Influencing is not a single-player game. It is a dynamic activity with multiple stakeholders.

❖ While business decisions may not always play a direct role in individual influencing goals, it is wise to weave the interests of the business into the influencing approach.

❖ Raising awareness is the first courageous step that you are taking towards influencing.

❖ Serial Influencers can use the strategies below to practice 'Awareness.'

1. *NAME THE EMOTIONS*

2. *KNOW YOUR CORE VALUES*

3. *IDENTIFY YOUR NICHE*

4. *SPEAK TO A NEUTRAL THIRD PARTY*

5. *OBSERVE NONVERBAL CUES*

6. *WALK IN THEIR SHOES*

7. *INVEST IN A SOPHISTICATED PERSONALITY ASSESSMENT TOOL*

8. *STAKEHOLDER ANALYSIS*

9. *CONNECT THE DOTS*

8: ARTICULATION

Articulation is an essential skill that can significantly impact various aspects of life, including professional success, personal relationships, and overall self-expression. As an Influencer, you often talk to multiple stakeholders to persuade them with your ideas.

In the previous section, we discussed Awareness and how it supports your influence strategy. The next step in building your Influencer's Language is Articulation. The ability to convey ideas is essential for persuading others or driving change. Influencers who articulate their thoughts effectively can inspire action and rally support for their ideas.

'Awareness' is a personal activity. It is the process of gathering the secret ingredients to draft effective messages. 'Articulation' is the **secret sauce** that converts your silent stakeholder observations and keen self-reflection into meaningful and impactful messages that influence your intended audience.

In short, Awareness + Articulation = Credibility

With all the groundworks that comes with observing your stakeholders, analyzing the power dynamics, and comprehending the business needs, you now have the next task of drafting and articulating a compelling message that gets buy-in from every one of your stakeholders as well as addresses the business challenges that they are trying to solve.

Clear articulation is critical. Period. When walking into the stakeholder's world, your observations are private. The stakeholders are most likely unaware of the research and preparation that you have invested in as a highly aware Influencer. **What the stakeholders experience is your articulation – it is their initial impression of you.**

Simply put, articulation is a branding activity. Good articulation will set the stage for effective influencing, while poor articulation will close the doors for any current or future persuasion or influence attempts. People quickly form judgments, primarily based on others' communication skills, because words have immense power to engage, inspire, and motivate large groups. They leave an impact, both tangible and intangible.

Articulate speakers can leave positive first impressions with careful preparation, which can open doors to social and professional opportunities. This is particularly important for Serial Influencers as they leverage articulation as the bedrock of healthy relationships. Speaking clearly and expressing oneself well fosters understanding which can strengthen connections with others. Also, 'Serial Influencing' is as much about listening and adapting as it is about articulating. Clear communication, consistent engagement, and genuine consideration of other people's needs will build a strong foundation to influence stakeholders and create a win-win situation.

A framework to help draft compelling articulation is incorporating the following components.

How to Articulate =

WHAT + WHY + WHO + WHEN

When do you need to articulate?

— One of the most common mistakes in influencing is when people jump the gun and start their articulation prematurely. Or they wait too long for the right moment. Don't over-engineer your strategy when talking about your objective and agenda.

— Pause. Reflect. Prepare. And wait for the right moment to influence your stakeholders. Not a moment too soon or too late.

What could you articulate?

— Talk about your proposed solutions.

— Highlight the benefits to various groups of people.

— Detail the mutual success.

— Share the cost of NOT acting.

— Discuss the execution plan.

Why should you articulate?

— Build relationships with a more extensive network of stakeholders.

— To ensure that there is an ethical win-win situation.

— To meet your influencing objectives.

— Gain credibility as a subject matter expert.

— To address the business problem(s).

— To meet your influencing objectives.

Who is your audience?

— Your primary stakeholders.

— Your future stakeholder - anyone might follow your influencing attempts and form initial impressions.

— Anyone your proposed solutions may impact.

Where should you articulate?

— Formal and schedules stakeholder meetings

— Impromptu meetings. Don't wait for formal meetings. Take your stakeholders out for lunch. Create opportunities where your stakeholders hear you articulate your well-thought-out solutions.

— Look for organic ways to continuously articulate and establish your credibility. Examples include logs, speaking engagements, and even posts on LinkedIn, which are great ways to contribute your thought leadership. It helps you remain current and relevant in the minds of your stakeholders.

SERIAL INFLEUNCERS' STRATEGIES TO PRACTICE ARTICULATION:

1. MIND YOUR LANGUAGE

Influencing stakeholders and business leaders requires tact and a targeted strategic approach. While the awareness strategies from the previous section can help provide insights into the stakeholders' needs and the business culture, you still need to draft a compelling message for your audience.

Choose your words carefully. Use terms that your audience will understand. **Avoid jargon and overly complex language unless necessary for the audience**. Tailoring your vocabulary to align with your stakeholders is the first step in preventing confusion or miscommunication.

An example I have noticed in the learning and development world is trainers and instructional designers discussing the Kirkpatrick Model with stakeholders as they launch a new program. Their articulation approach will include the science and definition behind the four levels of assessments, their sophisticated approach to incorporating the framework in creating learning experiences, and their commitment to developing insights and metrics using the same. While the Kirkpatrick model is a valid and reliable tool to assess the knowledge application and behavior change of learners, getting into the depth of explaining Level 1-4 assessments to Finance, IT, and other business stakeholders might not be the best way to engage or convince them to launch a new program.

I've noticed that many stakeholders lose interest in a few minutes as they shift in their seats or pull out their phones. At the end of the meeting, the questions from the few 'present' stakeholders were always about the ROI of this project. How long is the deployment time? Can we move this initiative to the next quarter?

In the above example, the Learning team need not oversimplify their approach but must simplify their narrative. **Respecting your stakeholders' intellect but not overburdening them with needless jargon is**

essential. The Learning team might be more successful with their stakeholders in relating their assessment process with tangible business outcomes and results without getting into the depth of describing and defining the Kirkpatrick model.

Similarly, I have seen business leaders' attention wander when the HR team discusses employee engagement or onboarding meetings. Most support functions are guilty of using fluffy language to describe their initiatives. However, the same business leaders will be alert as the HR team discusses compensation and recruiting strategy.

Incorporate business speak. This includes articulating a direct impact on the bottom line, profitability, and overall business vision. Your stakeholders want to know how your proposals and ideas will add value to the business operations. Make the stakeholders' jobs easy by providing the data and metrics that support the return on investment, the mutual benefits, and the success criteria of your proposal. Earn your stakeholders' respect as a credible Influencer; this will help turn decisions in your favor.

Avoid a lost-in-translation scenario by ensuring your articulation speaks to a broader audience. Take the example of HSBC, for example, when they had to rebrand their entire 'assume nothing' campaign because the slogan was interpreted as 'do nothing' in many countries, leading to a $10 million rebranding effort. Or when KFC's 'Finger Lickin' Good' was translated into Chinese as "Eat Your Fingers Off.'

In both scenarios, the company did not intend to offend or miscommunicate, but given the global complexities, it is inevitable that some messages will be lost in translation. You might also misunderstand or misinterpret when communicating with stakeholders across different cultures and regions.

Successful articulation is often about your continuous adaptation to meet the needs of your audience. Assume that your audience will need to learn what you mean precisely; be prepared to elaborate, and provide examples proactively, and pause frequently to check for alignment and agreement. Avoid situations where cultural or language nuances might get overlooked. Ask questions, seek guidance, and test your assumptions to remain culturally informed.

2. MAKE THEM AN OFFER THEY CAN'T REFUSE!

The Godfather knew the trick to make an offer one can't refuse.

As an Influencer, you can propose an attractive solution to your stakeholders. You can create a proposal that aligns well with the interests of your stakeholders so that they can't decline or disapprove of the most logical and advantageous solution provided to them.

To craft such an offer, **you must make it personal for every stakeholder involved**. The success of your articulation depends on how well you can relate the benefits of your ideas directly to your audience's personal or professional goals. For instance, the HR team can grab the attention of their audiences on even what most consider a fluffy topic if they can connect the program's goals to and attribute the program's success to the strong leadership of each of the stakeholder's departments. This example is a win-win situation that ensures continuous collaboration and partnership between the HR team and the business leaders.

Learn about your stakeholders' needs, wants, and pain points before making an offer that aligns with their deepest aspirations. Examples of such stakeholder aspirations include promotion, visibility, free time, more support, access to tools and platforms, etc. Curate your offer in such scenarios; a one-size-fits-all solution might not work. Highlight the benefits of your solution by clearly articulating tangible and relevant outcomes that might help your stakeholders attain their deepest aspirations. Be prepared to listen to any objections or concerns they may have and to adjust your offer accordingly. This approach shows you value their input and are willing to work towards a mutually beneficial agreement. Such offers are hard to refuse.

Making an irresistible offer as part of your influencing strategy is like *selling*. Consider what perks or bonuses will increase the value of your proposal without impacting the cost. Make your stakeholders feel special by suggesting that the offer is unique to them or only available to a select few.

As a learning and development leader, I often work with multiple stakeholders; influencing is a full-time job. I rely on crafting offers that are hard to refuse to accomplish my department's objective and build better relationships with my stakeholders. An example of irresistible offers I have proposed for my stakeholder groups is a customized learning dashboard as a value add to provide them with real-time metrics on the critical success metrics.

Another personal example is when leading leadership development programs, I intentionally restrict the number of participants and sessions for a few signature programs. I also incorporate a leadership nomination process to establish criteria and eligibility to participate in the program. I include unique markers or privileges for the program participants – retreats, North Face jackets, executive leadership meetings, and shadow opportunities to cement the unique and exclusive experiences. As a result of this approach, we have a long waiting list for the programs and never have to sell or promote the program actively.

Other strategies include incorporating testimonials, case studies, or endorsements to demonstrate that other stakeholders or external competitors have implemented and benefited. **Finally, make it easy for the stakeholders to say yes**. Simplify any processes or requirements that could create friction or delay acceptance. The easier it is to take advantage of the offer, the harder it will be to refuse your proposal.

Remember that an "offer they can't refuse" should never involve unethical practices, intimidation, or manipulation. At its best, it's about making an offer so well-suited to the other party's needs and interests that it naturally compels agreement.

3. The Science of Articulation

The science of articulation is straightforward, with **13 techniques** to craft and share your message effectively. To be successful, incorporate most techniques as often as possible or needed. And practice them without fail. Adopt them as habits for effective communication delivery.

— Speak clearly and concisely. Avoid filler words like "um," "like," and "you know." These can distract from your message and undermine your authority.

— Don't rush through your words. Speak at a measured pace to allow your listeners to absorb your words. Conversely, speaking too slowly can seem condescending or bore your audience.

— Use inflection and tone to add interest and emphasize important points. A monotone voice can make even exciting information seem dull.

— Speak loudly enough to be heard, but don't appear to be shouting. Modulate your volume to suit the setting and to emphasize key points.

— Practice breathing exercises to support your voice, especially before your pitch. Proper breathing can help control your pace and volume.

— Practice pronouncing names and terms, clearly and precisely. This is critical, especially with a global audience, as improper pronunciation can be distracting and make you appear less credible.

— Don't rush the pitch. Take strategic pauses to allow your points to sink in and to give yourself a moment to collect your thoughts.

— Demonstrate open and welcoming body language, facial expressions, and eye contact to convey your message and emotions.

— Know your pitch well. This includes the data, research, plans, etc. Familiarity with the content will allow you to focus more on how you are speaking.

— Maintain a conversational tone, even when speaking to a group. It can make your speech more relatable and understandable.

— Observe skilled speakers and incorporate their effective techniques into your speaking style.

— Get constructive feedback from others. Record your speeches or conversations to review your articulation.

— Believe in what you are saying. **Confidence can be heard in your voice and can persuade your audience.**

4. THE ART OF STORYTELLING

Great influencing strategies, successful negotiations, and impactful persuasion are centered on excellent storytelling. Most people hesitate to try storytelling; they might wonder if they have any good stories to share, might be unwilling to share personal details, or might worry if they have the skill sets to be powerful storytellers.

Powerful articulation is fundamental to influence successfully and repeatedly. Equally important is the ability to make lasting impressions on your stakeholders. Stanford research reported that messages with relevant data and metrics led to 5 to 10% retention. However, when anecdotes or great stories were added to the metrics, the retention rate increased to 65 - 70%.

Here are a few tips to incorporate storytelling in your influencing approach:

— <u>Story Bank</u>

To begin storytelling, take stock of your current story bank. If you don't have one, now is an excellent time to collect stories you can use at the workplace, not just for holiday gatherings. Stories can create connections between people. Your stories might reflect some of your wins, struggles, challenges, or learning. However, knowing your audience and understanding the context is vital before you leverage any of your stories to influence others.

Imagine a senior leader trying to influence his stakeholders, including his peers, senior leaders, and cross-functional leads, to launch a new tool requiring a steep learning curve and multiple process rework. The Influencer can lay out all the facts and data on the ROI and efficiency and make an irresistible offer that brings value to all stakeholders. Additionally, Influencers can share stories about themselves or others to enhance their influencing attempts. They can hook their stakeholders' attention and engagement by providing a relatable tale of similar people and similar events. Furthermore, they can embellish their story with vivid details on how the characters in the story found success and are reaping the benefits of their wise choices. Who doesn't like a success story?!

Storytelling can inspire a visual experience. In the above example, the stakeholders might forget the data, metrics, and timelines, but they will remember the picture you painted with relatable people.

— <u>Embellish; Don't lie.</u>

Storytelling intends to humanize you and your experiences. Great stories will pave the path to building credibility and relationships with your stakeholders. Don't ruin your efforts by articulating a hard-to-believe story. **While you might have to embellish specific details for humor** or increase the drama or tension, don't lie about critical information like numbers, data, or metrics. And keep sight of your ultimate objective - connecting with your stakeholders.

If you do not have a credible story or are unwilling to share personal details, don't hesitate to share a case study or example that you know has been successful. In such instances, highlight the people, their journey, business impact, and lessons learned rather than just the numbers.

In some scenarios, create a backup story with a fictional setting similar to the current situation and fictional characters that resemble your stakeholders. Articulate a compelling story to drive the right behaviors and actions that serve the stakeholders' interests and the business outcomes. **Practice the story**, especially if you are creating fictional stories. And remember to be ethical and avoid manipulating your stakeholders' emotions with a fictional story.

— <u>Identify the Intent.</u>

Before storytelling, be clear about what you want each stakeholder to do after hearing your message or stories. Do you want them to provide support, motivation, or inspiration to enable decision-making? Or do you want to highlight potential risks and challenges if the decision gets delayed? **Aligning on the ultimate message will** help you select the right story to move your audiences.

Finally, practice, practice, and practice. And allow your personality and authentic self to shine through.

5. ESTABLISH URGENCY

Establishing urgency in your articulation is similar to 'marketing' strategies. It creates a narrative that is action-driven and decision-oriented. Notice the store posters, banners, and even emails you receive from your favorite retail stores, such as "Limited Stock," "$9.99 today only", "Act Soon," "Running out of stock," or "Join the waitlist." These are curated narratives to get the buyers' (stakeholders') attention.

Research says that this method, where people want what is difficult to acquire, helps convert interest to purchasing options quickly.

You can apply the same principle when influencing your stakeholders. If you are sure of the value of your proposal or solutions, **use time-sensitive language to create a sense of urgency** while also describing the quick wins to the current problems. For example, "Time is running out to implement this new process flow; we can still save 10% of the overall projected cost" or "We might not receive another discount like this for another year; "accepting this price quote will still provide a small return on our investment."

Alternatively, explain what could happen if they don't act promptly, focusing on potential missed opportunities or worsening issues or examples of those who have faced setbacks due to hesitance. Align your proposals to a trending topic or a pressing business issue that requires immediate attention. An example could be to bring up competitor analysis when articulating, "Company A hesitated to incorporate security awareness policies leading to a massive security breach and client audits," or "We need a new retention strategy to identify the critical roles and talent before our attrition numbers get worse."

Finally, **give a clear deadline to add real-time pressure**. Commit to the deadline, and don't waver.

Make peace with the outcomes if they do not meet your objectives. Extending deadlines makes you appear less credible and will make it difficult for you to make an offer that's hard to refuse in the future.

Remember, while it's essential to create a sense of urgency, **it's equally important to maintain honesty and integrity in your approach**. Do not create false scarcity or exaggerate claims, as this can backfire even if one of your stakeholders challenges your scarcity claim and provides another viable option. Furthermore, it can make you appear inauthentic and erode the credibility you have built with your stakeholders.

6. TAILOR WITH STYLE

Your stakeholders at the workplace will likely have a wide range of communication styles and preferences. Your success as an Influencer depends on how well you can identify the motivation of your stakeholders and extend that knowledge to adapt your articulation, negotiation, persuasion, and influence techniques.

You can succeed as a serial Influencer who promotes cross-cultural understanding and collaboration across a broad and diverse set of stakeholders if you can incorporate different styles and respect your stakeholders' needs in this increasingly globalized world.

Pay attention to what your stakeholders value. What do they pay attention to the most? Examples include accuracy, data, stability, collaboration, execution plans, and business results. Connect with your stakeholders frequently to understand their value statements.

Tailor your content to reflect the stakeholder values and draft a message that resonates with your stakeholders.

For instance, if your stakeholder values accuracy and data, don't spend all your time discussing change management and collaboration. Or vice versa. You don't need to ignore the other values but wait until you build your credibility with this client with your tailored articulation before diving deep into other solution details.

Stakeholders can be judgmental. Especially when they don't receive or hear the message in a format they are accustomed to. Some stakeholders might process large files with complete project details, while others only need the headline and punchline. The business might be interested in the ROI and execution plan, while the primary stakeholders might be concerned about the impact on resource allocation and change management. Tailor your articulation regularly as you observe stakeholder dynamics. Be comfortable communicating with one-pagers, executive summaries, bullet-points or Excel project plans at any given time.

Invest in a behavioral assessment tool for you and your stakeholders, especially if you intend to influence a large group of people for extended periods. Wiley's DiSC assessment is one such assessment tool that'll provide you with insights into your stakeholders' motivators and derailers for effective communication and collaboration. Other examples include Enneagram, Typefinder and Clifton StengthsFinders.

8. ARTICULATION: COMMON MISTAKES

The importance of articulating cannot be overstated when it comes to influencing group(s) of people. It enhances personal and professional relationships, opens opportunities, and allows for effective exchange of ideas. Regular practice, active listening, and continuous adaptation can improve articulation skills over time. Be mindful of limiting your potential to articulate. Take care to avoid the following common mistakes.

Monotone articulation

Be expressive and connect emotionally. Stakeholders are more likely to be convinced if they feel an emotional connection. Brand your articulation style with data, metrics, relevant content, and storytelling.

Taking a one-size-fits-all approach

Research your stakeholders' needs and motivation.

Not practicing your pitch

Make sure to highlight the benefits, immediate benefits, and the consequences of inaction. Anticipate and prepare for counterarguments.

Overloading with information

Make sure to incorporate the stakeholders' communication style. Information can be shared over quick calls, formal meetings, lunch meetups, emails, and texts. Never underestimate the power of causal networking to distribute information.

Ignoring the context

Address the cross-cultural dynamics proactively and learn about the business direction for effective influencing.

Not speaking the business language

Avoid jargon and complex language that might confuse your audience. Use business-speak to convince your stakeholders and the business groups.

Not expanding your network

Influencing is not a one-off activity. Broaden your network and engage with existing and new stakeholders.

Not listening or observing

Stakeholders are constantly communicating. Pay attention to their reactions, especially when articulating.

Not being patient and persistent

Never miss an opportunity to demonstrate your expertise and your solutions in the best light possible. You'll need multiple attempts to build credibility. Don't give up too soon.

Not appreciating your stakeholders

Thank your stakeholders for their attention, engagement, and adoption of your idea. Continue learning and stay informed about stakeholders' needs and the business context. Continue updating your stakeholders with relevant information.

ARTICULATION TAKEAWAYS

❖ Influencers who articulate their thoughts effectively can inspire action and rally support for their ideas.

❖ 'Articulation' is the secret sauce that converts your silent stakeholder observations and keen self-reflection into meaningful and impactful messages that influence your intended audience.

❖ Awareness + Articulation = Credibility

❖ Your articulation creates your stakeholders' initial impression of you.

❖ Good articulation will set the stage for effective influencing, while poor articulation will close the doors for any current or future persuasion or influence attempts.

❖ Incorporate WHEN, WHAT, WHY, WHO & WHERE to draft a compelling message.

❖ Serial Influencers can use the strategies below to practice 'Articulation.'

1. *MIND YOUR LANGUAGE*

2. *MAKE THEM AN OFFER THEY CAN'T REFUSE*

3. *THE SCIENCE OF ARTICULATION*

4. *THE ART OF STORYTELLING*

5. *ESTABLISH URGENCY*

6. *TAILOR WITH STYLE*

9: ACTION

You've raised awareness about yourself and your stakeholders. You now understand the business goals and can customize your solutions to meet the influence outcomes. You've used your awareness to craft the right message for your audiences. You have impressed every one of your stakeholders. Your ideas were well received, and quick decisions were taken to approve your proposal. You've led the way to a great win-win situation.

So, what's next?

At this point, most people assume that the influencing approach was successful, and they wrap up their attempts to continue influencing after winning their stakeholder's approvals.

While the initial influencing approach might have been successful (or even unsuccessful), this is when serial influencing begins. Your opportunity to drive continuous impact, maintain credibility, and build partnerships with your stakeholders starts only now. In short, you are now moving toward becoming a **Serial Influencer.**

Let's consider how employees and leaders measure successful influence at work. Some long-term success indicators I've heard from professionals and leaders include:

— Establishing credibility.

— Achieving customer satisfaction.

— Gaining new business opportunities.

— Continuous collaboration and partnership.

— Transforming the business operations.

— Contributing to the company's overall performance profitability and the ability to meet strategic objectives.

Building credibility and establishing trust with peers, leaders, and the organizational community is essential for all the above.

As we discussed earlier, influencing is not a one-off activity. Before you know it, you will be in yet another scenario with the same or different stakeholders trying to influence them for another project. **Given the overlap and dependencies you might have with** your stakeholder networks at the workplace, you can never stop influencing. To maintain your momentum, reinforce your message, and scale the impact of your Influence, think about how you can continuously act to enhance your credibility and establish trust with your stakeholders.

Action speaks louder than words. While you might have dazzled, charmed, or impressed your stakeholders with your ideas and eloquent articulation tailored to their needs, the subsequent steps involve seamlessly blending your ideas and strategies. Your tactful execution will determine if your stakeholders will give you another opportunity to influence them.

Influencing in the workplace is often catering to repeat customers who might be in your sphere of Influence. **I recommend building a brand that inspires credibility, trust, and partnership with your stakeholders**. This will ensure your long-term success at any organization.

Scaling Influence is where I see most professionals struggle. Happy and easily satisfied with the success of their initial influencing attempts, only a few professionals put the same level of commitment and dedication into managing the execution of their proposals. Irrespective of your future success goals, as an Influencer, **you must continue after 'Articulation.'** Focus on establishing a more robust presence with your stakeholders and demonstrating accountability to see through your proposals and plans.

We will now discuss practical strategies to help develop an execution plan that will allow you to continue your influence attempts and devise a strategy that will pave the path toward better collaboration and trust with your stakeholders.

SERIAL INFLUENCERS' STRATEGIES TO PRACTICE ACTION:

1. DELIVER ON YOUR PROMISES TO YOUR STAKEHOLDERS & THE BUSINESS

Reliability and trustworthiness are critical components that help Influencer build strong professional relationships. To deliver on your promises to your stakeholders, you must **practice a strong accountability culture as an Influencer**. Taking ownership of your promises and holding yourself accountable for delivering them sets the stage for actively managing your stakeholders' expectations. This accountability mechanism will also include the responsibility for any setbacks and proactively visualizing solutions to overcome any obstacles.

As the Influencer, ownership begins with you. By demonstrating active ownership, you become the brand ambassador of the project. Such active ownership will also help build the credibility of the Influencer as a passionate champion.

Below are some practices you can adopt to hold yourself accountable.

— Define your commitments with the stakeholders to ensure they are specific and measurable. You need to have complete clarity on the commitments you have made to the stakeholders. This will help you hold yourself accountable for achieving the specific objectives.

— Develop a detailed plan to outline the steps you need to take to deliver on your promises and set deadlines to establish structure and priority for yourself before you bring it to your team or the stakeholders. Follow this activity with a logical execution plan that we will discuss in the upcoming steps.

— Define clear metrics and indicators that demonstrate whether you have fulfilled your promises. Examples of such metrics could be reaching specific milestones, outcomes accomplished, time to accomplish etc.

— Set aside time for regular self-reflection to assess your progress. Identify what went well and areas of improvement to adjust your approach as needed.

— Celebrate your success when you deliver on your promises, as recognizing and rewarding your accomplishments can reinforce positive behaviors and motivate you to maintain high levels of accountability in the future.

— Request feedback from colleagues and other peers. Get constructive feedback, which will provide valuable insights to help you refine your accountability strategies.

You need to demonstrate accountability with your stakeholders as well. A few tips to establish accountability with your stakeholders are:

- Keep stakeholders informed about your progress through open and honest communication.

- Share bad news immediately. This includes delays, potential barriers, or obstacles.

- Seek feedback from your stakeholders to understand if their expectations are being met. And if your stakeholders have any suggestions for improvement.

- Share success stories with your stakeholders. Spotlight rockstar performances from your team, where applicable.

Finally, leverage accountability as your brand identity to reassure your stakeholders that you are taking ownership to meet your commitments.

2. FUNDAMENTAL PROJECT PLAN FOR YOUR TEAM

To state the obvious, a structured execution plan will provide a roadmap for achieving your objectives efficiently. **Planning for such execution involves meticulous attention to detail and a proactive approach to identifying and addressing potential challenges**. Here are some essential steps to prepare for flawless execution:

— Clearly understand and list the goals of the influence outcome. Break down the goals into smaller tasks or actions that need to be completed. These tasks should directly contribute to the achievement of the overall goal. For instance, the outcome of the

Influence might be that the Influencer receives approval to enroll in a certification program. The sub-tasks and actions include the timeline to prepare and take the certification, training, payments, etc.

Let's consider a complex goal – launching a new ticketing tool. The tasks may include procurement of the tool, change management, training, process remapping, testing, etc. As an Influencer, list all the potential tasks associated with your goal, regardless of complexity.

— Determine team members responsible for each task. For instance, in the above ticketing tool example, the Influencer must consider the team's capacity when delegating responsibilities. This activity will also help the Influencer identify the resources, such as budget, people, or tools needed to accomplish each task.

Influencers can leverage the following questions to establish the initial structure:

> What are the different tasks associated with this goal?

> Who can I delegate these tasks to?

> Does the current team have the skill set to complete these tasks?

> ➤ Does the current team have the availability to complete these tasks?

> ➤ Do I have enough people resources?

> ➤ Can I borrow resources from another team to complete this project?

> ➤ How can I set up cross-functional collaboration?

— Establish **realistic deadlines** for each task. Consider the interdependencies between tasks and allocate time accordingly. Ensure that this deadline will also meet the expectations of your stakeholders and the business.

— Implement a system for regular **process tracking**. Even in the certification example above, the Influencer must monitor their progress against the established tasks and milestones. Setting up this accountability mechanism is critical for any individual or group project.

— **Communicate the execution plan** to all team members involved. Ensure that everyone understands their roles, responsibilities, and the overall timeline. Additionally, meet with the project team regularly to:

- Seek feedback on their alignment with the plan and any proposed suggestions for enhancements.
- Communicate transparently on the status of the project and stakeholder expectations.
- Anticipate potential points of failure and develop contingency plans to mitigate risks.

- Address unforeseen challenges that arise. And adjust deadlines, reallocate resources, or revise tasks as necessary.
- Identify lessons learned and adjust the plan based on real-time insights and feedback.

— Develop robust **contingency plans for potential disruptions or unexpected events**. This could include alternative resource sources, backup suppliers, emergency protocols, or alternative workflows.

— **Integrate quality assurance measures** into the execution plan to ensure the deliverables meet the standards. Depending on the project, this can include regular quality checks, peer reviews, dry runs, pilot programs, and testing processes.

— Incorporate a comprehensive **debriefing methodology** to assess the outcomes and identify successes, challenges, and areas for improvement in future executions.

By integrating these steps into the planning process, you can set the stage for the flawless execution of your projects and initiatives. Each step plays a crucial role in **mitigating risks, maintaining quality, and ensuring that the execution plan is implemented with precision and excellence.**

3. TACKLE OBSTACLES

As an Influencer, you will likely face obstacles in meeting your objectives, especially after you start executing your solutions. Handling impediments as part of your influencing strategy is critical in ensuring your success and professional growth. Obstacles can take many forms, such as tool constraints, technology challenges, communication issues, time constraints, lack of resources, changing business direction, or any other unexpected setbacks. How you handle these obstacles can significantly impact the execution of your solution and your stakeholder's trust in your capabilities.

Addressing obstacles head-on can prevent minor issues from escalating into more significant problems. By anticipating, acknowledging, and tackling these challenges, you can minimize their impact on your work and stop them from derailing the overall progress of your projects. This proactive mindset will be perceived positively by the business and the stakeholders. Your approach might demonstrate your resilience and practical problem-solving skills, which are highly valued in the workplace.

Moreover, **overcoming obstacles increases your self-confidence**. Each time you or your team successfully navigates a challenge, you develop a greater sense of competence and resourcefulness. It also creates a learning opportunity leading to personal and professional growth, expanding your skill set, and increasing your value with your network.

Successfully navigating obstacles **can lead to greater recognition and advancement** within the organization. You are more likely to gain the trust of your stakeholders, which leads to increased responsibilities or opportunities for career advancement. More importantly, tackling obstacles effectively enhances your brand identity as a Serial Influencer.

As discussed, handling obstacles requires resilience, resourcefulness, and problem-solving skills. You can also use the techniques below to practice managing obstacles proactively.

Conduct a pre-mortem

This strategy will help you **anticipate potential failures or challenges** even before they happen. I suggest that you bring a group of people (supporters, critics, skeptics etc.) together to understand what potential concerns you should anticipate as you execute the project plan. Leverage your peers or team members as devil's advocates to play out multiple scenarios to understand the potential implications of any decisions made during the execution phase. This approach can help you proactively address risks and weaknesses before they become critical issues.

List it

You are likely overwhelmed with details and deadlines if you work on multiple projects and tasks. List every possible project and task you are working on to overcome this challenge. Next, select the line items with no obstacles and remove them from the list. Group the remaining tasks by the intensity and ambiguity of the challenges that you are anticipating or experiencing. Start identifying the resources you'll need and your next steps against each task. **The very act of creating this final list will help you stay focused and reduce any sense of anxiety that you might be experiencing.**

Whiteboard

Take problem-solving to the next level by getting your team members or peers together in a meeting room.

Brainstorm and whiteboard to discuss various approaches to solve your obstacles.

For instance, I have used large conference rooms and assigned each team member a specific whiteboard section. I set the agenda of the meeting to ideate and come up with individual solutions for the initial part of the meeting. Next, we get back together as a group and brainstorm on the benefits and features of every solution on the whiteboard. Creativity unlocks various approaches to solving any obstacles you or your team members might face.

You can try this activity using Zoom video conferencing if needed. You can also use this approach if you are brainstorming all by yourself. A visual creative activity helps reduce any sense of anxiety team members, or you might be experiencing.

Fail-Fast

The fail-fast approach is an excellent method to innovate, adapt, and learn in a dynamic marketplace. This concept encourages rapid experimentation, intending to identify failures early, minimize risk, and optimize learning. **Failing fast can help identify potential pitfalls and roadblocks early in the process, allowing for course correction and risk mitigation before investing time or resources.**

Influencers can use this method to run pilots and test scenarios. This will help them identify what works and doesn't, leading to better-informed decision-making.

It also helps save time and resources by avoiding prolonged investments in projects that may not be viable.

For instance, the new IT tool project can benefit from this strategy as the Influencer tests functionalities with a select audience in Phase I. They can take the lessons learned to refine their approach and project plan before investing more resources.

However, the fail-fast strategy will backfire without an accountability mechanism for continuous improvement and a focus on learning from failures. And only some projects or solutions could use the fail-fast method. However, when used responsibly, this approach can help you gain new perspectives and help prevent or manage obstacles in the long run.

4. GAIN YOUR STAKEHOLDERS' TRUST

Trust building is an ongoing process that requires continuous effort and commitment. Different stakeholders may have unique needs and expectations, so it is essential to adapt your approach to build trust with each group. Finally, trust takes time, so patience and persistence are key.

Earlier this section, we reviewed many strategies that address the 'Action' portion of Influence. Here is the summary of strategies to gain trust with your stakeholders:

Open and Honest Communication: Engage in open and honest communication with your stakeholders.

Share information proactively, address concerns transparently, and provide regular updates on progress and challenges. Clear and consistent communication can help build trust by keeping stakeholders informed and involved.

Consistency: Consistently delivering on promises and demonstrating reliability over time is critical to building trust. Be consistent in your actions, decisions, and communication. This helps stakeholders feel confident in their ability to follow through on commitments.

Integrity and Ethics: Demonstrating integrity, ethical behavior, and values-aligned decision-making is critical for building trust. Upholding these standards builds confidence in your actions and decisions.

Setting Clear Expectations: Clearly outline what stakeholders can expect from your relationship engagement and what you expect from them in return. Setting clear, realistic expectations can help avoid misunderstandings and build trust.

Relationship Building: Invest time and effort in building relationships with your stakeholders. Understand their needs, concerns, and expectations, and demonstrate empathy and a genuine interest in their perspectives. Building solid relationships fosters trust and collaboration.

<u>Accountability</u>: Take ownership of your actions and decisions. If mistakes are made, be accountable and transparent in addressing them. How you handle challenges and failures can significantly impact stakeholder trust.

<u>Ask for Feedback</u>: Address stakeholder concerns, feedback, and suggestions. Demonstrating that their voices are heard and valued and taking appropriate action in response can strengthen trust and demonstrate your commitment.

<u>Consensus Building</u>: Build consensus and find win-win solutions before conflicts arise. Building consensus demonstrates a commitment to

collaborative problem-solving and can strengthen stakeholder trust.

Empowerment and Involvement: Involve stakeholders in decision-making processes and projects where appropriate. Empowering stakeholders to contribute and be part of the process fosters a sense of ownership and trust.

Maintaining stakeholder trust requires a multifaceted approach emphasizing communication, responsiveness, integrity, and relationship building. By focusing on these areas and adapting your approach to meet the specific needs of your stakeholders, you can work toward building stronger, more trusting relationships.

ACTION TAKEAWAYS:

❖ Influencing is not a one-off activity. Building credibility and establishing trust with peers, leaders, and the organizational community is essential to becoming a Serial Influencer.

❖ Influencing in the workplace often caters to repeat customers who might be in your sphere of Influence.

❖ Action speaks louder than words. While you might have dazzled, charmed, or impressed your stakeholders with your ideas and eloquent articulation tailored to their needs, the subsequent steps involve seamlessly blending your ideas and strategies.

❖ Scaling Influence is where most professionals struggle.

❖ Your tactful execution will determine if your stakeholders give you another opportunity to influence them.

❖ Serial Influencers can use the strategies below to practice 'Action.'

1. *DELIVER ON YOUR PROMISES TO YOUR STAKEHOLDERS.*

2. *FUNDAMENTAL PROJECT PLAN FOR YOUR TEAM.*

3. *TACKLE OBSTACLES.*

4. *GAIN YOUR STAKEHOLDERS' TRUST.*

10: AMPLIFICATION

Amplifying your Influencer efforts will solidify your position as an expert in your niche and establish your identity as a trusted and valued partner with your stakeholders. In these digital post-pandemic times, the workplace is hybrid. Your stakeholders are dispersed across various locations and geographies. You might likely never meet your stakeholders in-person. The importance of communicating clearly and consistently has never been more critical. Influencers must showcase their expertise, value, and results to a global audience.

In this competitive landscape, being a *Serial Influencer* will help you stand out from the od

Occasional Influencers. Highlighting your differentiators, such as deep expertise, trusted partnership, innovative solutions, persistent problem-solving, and adaptability, will help you differentiate yourself from others in your organization and industry.

Being intentional about amplifying your influence efforts will enable you to inspire and impact many others, whether seeking to advocate for change, share knowledge, or drive for value-added solutions. You can attract like-minded individuals, enthusiastic collaborators, and invested sponsors and champions who will enable you to scale your influence efforts.

Amplifying your influence efforts is a strategic approach that leaves lasting and positive impressions on your stakeholders, making it an invaluable asset in the entire approach to becoming a serial Influencer. Your expertise and reputation will drive impact and build the foundation for sustained career success.

There are many success indicators to outline the traits of a successful Influencer. As discussed in the earlier chapters, these traits include self-awareness, stakeholder analysis, clear communication, transparency, high ethical standards, etc.

What sets apart a *Serial Influencer* from a *Good Influencer* is the investment they make towards the 'Awareness', 'Articulation', 'Action', and

'Amplification' sections of the Serial Influencer Model, which binds the various strategies from the earlier chapters and scales the effort of the Influencer across the company.

Serial Influencer who 'Amplify' their influence approach are often described as:

Visionary:

Influencers who can see beyond the present and visualize an impactful tomorrow are invariably Serial Influencers. They are driven by their desire to shape and influence what lies ahead with their long-term goals and aspirational outcomes. They align their vision with the greater good, seeking to create a positive impact and address the business or industry challenges.

Innovative:

Influencers who leverage a creative mindset to envision new ideas, solutions, or ways of thinking are invariably Serial Influencers. They are willing to challenge conventional ideas and are comfortable with uncertainty while pursuing innovation. They are curious and are constantly learning to keep up with the industry and market trends.

Adaptive:

Influencers who remain resilient in the face of any obstacles or industry shifts are invariably Serial Influencers. They establish a strong foundation for themselves and their teams to solve problems, anticipate future trends, and develop plans to reach their influencing goals.

Consistent:

Influencers who are consistently driving business outcomes and stakeholder engagements at EVERY instance are invariably Serial Influencers. Whether providing high-quality and reliable information or maintaining stakeholder relationships, they are consistently transparent, relatable, and genuine in their interactions with their audience.

Passionate:

Serial Influencers are passionate experts in their niche or area of expertise. Their enthusiasm resonates with their audience and drives engagement as they continue influencing the company and the industry.

Collaborators:

Influencers who intentionally collaborate with their teams, peers, and cross-functional leaders are invariably Serial Influencers. They optimize collaboration to bring diverse perspectives and expand the reach of their solutions.

SERIAL INFLUENCERS' STRATEGIES TO PRACTICE AMPLIFICATION:

1. ADAPT

Influence begins with raising awareness of your stakeholders' objectives and business needs and adapting your proposed solutions for a mutually beneficial outcome. As a serial Influencer, you can amplify your efforts by being adaptive. This includes adapting to the current market and industry trends, the evolving needs of your stakeholders, and the strategic shifts in business direction. Listed are a few methods to continuously adapt as you amplify your influence approach:

Stay informed about the latest market and industry developments by:

— Reading relevant industry publications.

- Attending conferences and seminars in your area of expertise.

- Subscribing to business magazines such as Harvard Business Review and The Economist.

- Attending networking events with other professionals in your fields.

— Being Curious

- Talking to your competitors to learn more about their approach.

- Reading case studies.

- Shadowing other Influencers.

INNOVATE TO DIFFERENTIATE

As a serial Influencer, you must differentiate yourself at the workplace as you continue to influence your stakeholders by establishing your brand as an invaluable asset to the company. You will gain immense traction with your stakeholders in influencing attempts by championing innovation and differentiation. Below are a few suggestions for adopting innovation and differentiation.

Continue to hone your craft as in Influencer to elevate your skills and expertise, ultimately positioning yourself as a leader in your field in your field. Some tips to hone your craft are:

— Stay up to date with the latest developments and best practices in your field. Examples include incorporating GenAI or technology trends.

— Connect with industry leaders who can provide guidance and mentorship. Learn from their experiences, seek advice, and leverage their insights to advance your expertise.

— Commit to ongoing education through workshops, online courses, industry certifications, and mentorship programs.

— Look for opportunities to practice what you've learned. Take on challenging projects, volunteer for new initiatives, and actively seek out tasks that allow you to practice and refine your skills.

— Teach and share to deepen your own understanding of a subject. Offer to mentor junior colleagues or present on topics related to your expertise. Teaching reinforces your own knowledge and provides an opportunity for feedback.

Mastery takes time and effort. Stay passionate about your craft and pursue excellence, even in the face of challenges or setbacks.

2. EXPAND YOUR NETWORK

A common mistake Influencers make is focusing on a narrow group of stakeholders. Given the dynamic shifts in the organization and marketplace, it is critical to build a strong network of stakeholders continuously. As an Influencer, practice observing verbal and non-verbal cues across multiple stakeholders to create a relationship with each of them proactively. This will enable you to gain new perspectives and learn about business priorities in advance. Establishing credibility and gaining the trust of multiple stakeholders over an extended period will amplify your influencing approach.

You can use the tips below to expand your networks.

— Leverage social media platforms such as LinkedIn to connect with professionals in your field. Engage in industry-related discussions to share content and connect with thought leaders.

— Engage in volunteer activities and community events. This can create opportunities to meet new people and expand your network while contributing to meaningful causes.

— Leverage your current contacts and stakeholders for introductions within their network.

— Stay in touch with former peers, classmates, and industry contacts. I make it a habit to contact at least one former colleague every month. Regular communication helps nurture professional future relationships and securing other potential opportunities.

— Participate in relevant online communities and forums related to your industry. Engage in discussions and share insights as you connect with others who share your interests.

— Participate in alumni networking events, if possible.

Building and expanding your network takes time and effort. You must nurture and maintain these relationships you build over time to provide genuine and authentic value to your stakeholders.

3. COLLABORATE

Influencing is a team sport. And to successfully influence, your reputation as a collaborative Influencer is critical to your success. Promoting an influence approach centered on teamwork and mutual support will enhance productivity and innovation.

As an Influencer, you are constantly striving to meet your objectives and those of your stakeholders. As a serial Influencer, you are a conscious and deliberate collaborator leading by example to set a standard for collaborative behavior within the company.

You can use the following tips to amplify collaboration in your influencing strategy.

— Create an environment where team members feel comfortable expressing their ideas, sharing feedback, and taking calculated risks without fear of negative consequences. This psychological safety encourages open communication and promotes trust within the team in the long term.

— Facilitate collaboration across different departments, functional areas, and geographical locations. Encouraging cross-cultural and cross-functional teamwork provides diverse perspectives and expertise, leading to a more comprehensive and innovative solution.

- Provide training on collaborative skills, conflict resolution, and effective communication. Building these competencies among team members and stakeholders can improve their ability to work cohesively.

- Spotlight your peers. In our earlier chapters, we discussed recognizing and rewarding team members who support the delivery of your solution. It is equally important to acknowledge your peers and stakeholders. This will secure more buy-in from your stakeholders as they receive acknowledgment of their input and value.

- Become a visible collaborator. Go above and beyond to provide your time and resources to your team and to your stakeholders.

— Encourage collaboration through social time. Casual conversations, team-building activities, lunches, dinners, and happy hours can all help foster stronger relationships, which can translate into better collaboration.

— Leverage technology and tools that streamline the collaboration process. This might include project management tools, messaging apps, and latest software with collaborative features that promote transparency and trust.

— Establish collaboration champions who exemplify nuanced collaborative skills. They can serve as mentors, advocates, and role models for effective collaboration.

— Incentivize collaboration efforts through awards and monetary prizes. Acknowledging and celebrating successful collaborative projects motivates team members and stakeholders to actively engage in future projects.

4. CONSTANTLY DO <u>MORE</u>

Consistently seeking ways to be better at influencing others requires dedication, self-awareness, and a commitment to continuous growth. By integrating the tips below into your influence approach, you can cultivate a culture of ongoing improvement and meaningful progress.

— More listening. As your network group expands and your amplification efforts accelerate, you must observe and expand your awareness.

- More networking and collaboration.

- More motivation to sustain your drive for improvement.

- More mentorship from experienced leaders in your field.

- More self-reflection to identify your areas of improvement.

- More continuous feedback from peers and mentors. Don't stop asking for feedback.

- More technology adoption relevant to your field to enhance the efficiency and effectiveness of your serial influencing approach.

- More stretch assignments to help you acquire new skills and demonstrate your capabilities.

- More time management to prioritize tasks and optimize productivity.

- More learning to stay updated on industry trends.

- Finally, more time. More investment. More people. More options. More innovation. More networking.

Keep asking, 'What else can I do?' to sustain the engagement with your stakeholders.

Amplification Takeaways:

❖ In this competitive landscape, being a Serial
Influencer will help you stand out from the od
Occasional Influencers

❖ Amplifying your influence efforts is a strategic
approach that leaves lasting and positive
impressions on your stakeholders, making it an
invaluable asset in the entire approach to
becoming a serial Influencer.

❖ What sets apart a Serial Influencer from a
Good Influencer is the investment they make
towards the 'Awareness,'' 'Articulation,''
'Action,'' and 'Amplification' sections of the
Serial Influencer Model

❖ Serial Influencer who 'Amplify' their influence approach are often described as 'Visionary,' 'Innovative, 'Adaptive,' 'Consistent,' 'Passionate,' and 'Collaborators.'

❖ Serial Influencers can use the strategies below to practice 'Amplification.'

1. *ADAPT*

2. *INNOVATE TO DIFFERENTIATE*

3. *EXPAND YOUR NETWORK*

4. *COLLABORATE*

5. *CONSTANTLY DO MORE*

11: QUICK CHECK!

Are you an Influencer or a Serial Influencer? Review the following influencing strategies we discussed in the earlier chapters.

In the table below, use a check mark to indicate how often you demonstrate the 24 Serial Influencer Strategies.

	Never	Sometimes	Always
AWARENESS			
Name the Emotion			
Know Your Core Values			
Identify Your Niche			
Speak to a Neutral 3rd Party			
Observe Nonverbal Cues			
Walk in their Shoes			
Invest in a Sophisticated Personality Assessment Tool			
Stakeholder Analysis			
Connect the Dots			
ARTICULATION			
Mind Your Language			
Make Them an Offer They Can't Refuse			
The Science of Articulation			
The Art of Storytelling			
Establish Urgency			
Tailor with Style			
ACTION			
Deliver on Your Promises			
Fundamental Project Plan			
Tackle Obstacles			
Gain Your Stakeholders' Trust			
AMPLIFICATION			
Adapt			
Innovate to Differentiate			
Expand Your Network			
Collaborate			
Constantly Do More			

Consider the following reflection questions to develop your influencing approach.

— What do you think?

— Are you an Influencer or a Serial Influencer?

— What are your strengths?

— Areas of opportunity?

— What is your plan to adopt new strategies?

Conclusion

Thank you for purchasing and reading this book. I hope you enjoyed reading the book. And I hope the book helped you understand the importance of becoming a Serial Influencer.

Influencing is not easy; it is an enormous responsibility. Driving better outcomes for yourself, your stakeholders, and the business requires intentional practice. In my last 20 years of leading talent functions, I have realized that influencing is the most critical skill for any professional and leader. And it is vital to constantly upgrade your influencing skills to meet the needs of the ever-evolving talent marketplace.

I've shared tips and strategies that I have used in my journey to become a Serial Influencer. I consciously practice these strategies in each of my influencing efforts across various global stakeholders. These strategies help me stay focused and grounded on understanding my stakeholders and business needs. I hope this book helps you refine your influencing strategies that you can implement with your stakeholder groups.

I'd love to hear about your story and insights. Please feel free to e-mail me at

akkshada.maniyan@gmail.com

Resources

Sign up for a free Masterclass on Serial Influencing.

Please use the link below to indicate your interest. Session information and calendar details will follow upon submission.

Link: https://shorturl.at/aryJ1

About the Author

Leveraging two decades of expertise in coaching, talent development, and people operations, Akkshada Maniyan leads Learning and Organizational Development for Innova Solutions.

Akkshada's influence spans from emerging professionals to senior leaders across diverse industries, equipping over 50,000 learners with the tools to lead with purpose in a rapidly changing world.

As a Columbia University Certified Executive Coach, Akkshada's mission is to inspire and empower leaders to future-proof their careers and drive meaningful change in themselves and their communities.

She regularly shares her thoughts on leadership, change, and curiosity with followers across various platforms.